Masonry's Secret Legends

I0102478

Also from Westphalia Press

westphaliapress.org

Masonry's Secret Legends

Volume 3, Number 1 of
Ritual, Secrecy, and Civil Society

Edited by Pierre Mollier

WESTPHALIA PRESS
An imprint of Policy Studies Organization

Masonry's Secret Legends:
Volume 3, Number 1 of Ritual, Secrecy and Society
All Rights Reserved © 2016 by Policy Studies Organization

Westphalia Press
An imprint of Policy Studies Organization
1527 New Hampshire Ave., NW
Washington, D.C. 20036
info@ipsonet.org

ISBN-13: 978-1-63391-502-2
ISBN-10: 1-63391-502-6

Cover design by Taillefer Long at Illuminated Stories:
illuminatedstories.com

Daniel Gutierrez-Sandoval, Executive Director
PSO and Westphalia Press

Updated material and comments on this edition
can be found at the Westphalia Press website:
www.westphaliapress.org

Ritual, Secrecy, and Civil Society
Volume 3, Number 1 • Spring 2015
©2015 Policy Studies Organization

Table of Contents

Ritual, Secrecy and Civil Society:
Issue No. 5, Summer 2015

Freemasonry and its Legends: Between the Orient and Scotland

Foreword by Pierre Mollier, Editor-in-Chief

Thanks to the work of David Stevenson concerning Scotland in the seventeenth century, and to those of the research Lodge of the *Quatuor Coronati*, relating to England in the early eighteenth century, we know a little better how speculative freemasonry originated. However, aside from the chain of events that led to the creation of the modern Lodges, then the Grand Lodges, we still need to understand the origin of the intellectual and legendary corpus that they employed and which forged the masonic identity. In France, Christelle Imbert and Hugues Berton have just published a major work on this question. In *Les enfants de Salomon: Approches historiques et rituelles sur les compagnonnages et la franc-maçonnerie* (Paris: Dervy, 2015), they lay before us a vast study of close or more distant sources, as well as the symbolic figures and themes used in masonic rituals and instructions. It is a study based on a very large number of documents, some of which are very rare. In this book, they offer us the fruit of their research into these "Liberal Arts" which already featured prominently in the *Old Charges* of the Middle Ages and which were to be found in the masonic texts of the eighteenth and nineteenth centuries. We see clearly how the roots of the masonic acacia reach back into ancient times.

Freemasonry and the Stuarts is considered a subject of legend by most serious masonic historians! Yet, *in fine*, there was a real and well documented example when Charles Edward Stuart accepted, then laid claim to, the office of Grand Master of the Order! This is quite a fascinating case where the strength of an idea—originally false, we must admit—in the end created a reality. For a historian, a false idea which is widespread is a true fact. Besides, this rather strange affair leads us into the subtleties of masonic geo-politics during the Enlightenment.

Besides the *Craft*, the high degrees are an important aspect of masonic practice and have been since the eighteenth century, although very often masonic organizations tend to sideline them. The history of the high degrees has progressed considerably in recent years. However, one question remains quite obscure, that being their origins and the appearance of the very first high degrees. Based on the recent work of some of our colleagues, we believe we can now advance a hypothesis as to the appearance of the "first" high degree.

Alongside the issues inherent in masonic history, *Ritual, Secrecy and Civil Society* seeks to examine the influence and roles of freemasonry in various areas of intellectual, artistic or social life. This is why we are particularly delighted to publish the second part of the magnificent study by Thierry Zarcone on the links between freemasonry and the beginnings of modern orientalism. Apart from the academic interest of this contribution to the history of human sciences, it contains such colorful characters!

doi: 10.18278/rscs.3.1.1

The Liberal Arts and the English Old Charges

Hugues Berton and Christelle Imbert[A]

The English Old Charges[1], or Ms. Constitutions, are texts in manuscript presented in the form of vellum sheets or, for the oldest of them, in scrolls. There are also printed versions from the eighteenth century onward. They consist essentially of a statement of the rules relating to the professional conduct of a mason, preceded by a prayer, a description of the Liberal Arts, and the legendary history of the passing on of the profession of mason. They do not contain any element of ritual, except that the commitment by oath is done by placing one's hand on the Book.[2] The nature of this book is not specified. It could be the Bible. However, one single document indicates that the oath should be sworn on "the Holy Contents of this Roll" (Rawlinson Ms., 1700–1750).

No other profession in Great Britain has documents similar to these referring to a legendary origin. Although there are variations, they contain a common thread and it is likely that each British lodge in operation would have a copy, as they were read to an apprentice when he was received: "King Athelstan . . . commanded that it should be readd or tould, when that any Mason should be made", (Dowland Ms., 1550, published in 1815, and subsequent manuscripts).

We are currently aware of some 110 copies listed under the name of Old Charges; others have disappeared, "having been too hastily burned by some over-conscientious brothers," according to claims by Anderson (Constitutions, 1738). The oldest dates from 1390 (Regius Ms.), and the most recent from the beginning of the nineteenth century. They are arranged in families and branches according to their origins and convergences.

The Old Charges were initially a feature of English Freemasonry, but they seem to have been used in Scotland from 1660, then from 1710 associated with Scottish catechisms (Dumfries Ms. No. 4), and finally taken up and enhanced in Anderson's Constitutions of 1723.

The only two texts we have from the medieval period are the Ms. Regius (c. 1390) and the Ms. Cooke (c. 1410), probably written by clerks for whom the masons were still working, during the Hundred Years War (1337–1475). At that time the construction of large religious buildings was still continuing apace in England. One needs only note the building of King's College, Cambridge around 1450. Then there is

---

[A] Hugues Berton and Christelle Imbert have just published *Les Enfants de Salomon* (Paris: Editions Dervy, 2015). This contribution is taken from this work.

[1] For the dating of the Old Charges manuscripts, we are following the list updated in 1986 by the historian Wallace Mac Leod, which we give in the appendix of our work, according to family and branch of membership.

[2] This procedure is given in Latin in the text: "*Tunc unus ex senioribus teneat librum ut ille vel illi potiat vel potiant manus sup librum et tunc precepta deberent Legi*" (Watson Ms., 1687), and also found in later documents.

doi: 10.18278/rscs.3.1.2

nothing for almost 150 years, and it is only from the second half of the sixteenth century that we see new examples of the texts of the Old Charges.

The Anglican Reform that began in 1534 may have caused revisions to be made to the Old Charges which followed, of which one may have acted as a model for later manuscripts such as the Dowland (c. 1550–1815), Lansdowne (c. 1600), Grand Lodge No. 1 (1583) and York No. 1 (1600) manuscripts. In the seventeenth century, despite the gradual disappearance of operating lodges, many Old Charges were drawn up which referred to medieval origins. They may have been an essential element in the reception of the first non-operating masons, such as Elias Ashmole in Warrington in 1646.

Following the Great Fire of London in 1666, building in stone became much prized and the organization of the profession underwent a restructuring. In the early eighteenth century, new text structures appeared in the form of catechisms, influenced by those in Scotland, and they co-existed with the Old Charges for almost a century, before replacing them. These versions show increasing emphasis on ethical standards in relation to individuals rather than to the profession.

All the Old Charges have a similar structure. They start and end with a specific prayer. Then there is a description of the liberal arts, followed by the legendary story of the origin of Freemasonry. The Old Charges also contain obligations, and a declaration of the material and ethical rules concerning the practice of the profession, as well as the oath to be sworn by each member.

The Liberal Arts

The Old Charges contain an invitation to discover the origin of Freemasonry and of the Liberal Arts: "Good Brethren and Followes: Our purpose is to tell you how and in what manner this worthy science of Masonrye was begunne, and afterwards how it was favoured by worthy Kings and Princes, and by many other worshippfull men."[3] "Ye shall understand that there be seven liberal sciences, by the which seven all sciences and crafts, in the world, were first found, and in especiall for he is causer of all, that is to say the science of geometry of all other that be, the which seven sciences are called thus."[4]

We are going to examine certain aspects of the seven sciences or liberal arts (from *liber*, book) in the Old Charges. The teaching of the Liberal Arts was initially part of the syllabus for educated people in the Middle Ages. In the practice of Operative Masonry, they constituted a yardstick for any mason who wished to do his job well, and gave rise to detailed instructions. Far from being just a list, as is the case in Speculative Masonry, they introduced the practical side necessary in the art of building. Medieval operative masons would therefore absorb the Liberal Arts, and memorize their applications.

We should first look back at the origins of the teaching of the Liberal Arts and their implications in Antiquity and in the Middle Ages.

Book 7 of Plato's *Republic*, written around 354 BC, begins with an exposition of the Allegory of the Cave. Man first becomes aware of his state of confinement and illusion: if he is freed from his chains, and forced to stand up and turn towards

---

[3] Dowland Ms. (1550).
[4] Cooke Ms. (1410).

the light, he suffers from being dazzled. It is only by becoming gradually accustomed to the light that he will be able to make out first the shadows, then the objects themselves. Later, he will be able to look at the heavenly bodies at night and the sky itself, then the sun in its true place, as it is. Plato states that "the ascent and the contemplation of the things above" is to be considered like "the soul's ascension to the intelligible region."[5] Once this experience of divine contemplation has been completed, he should descend "again among the bondsmen and share their labours and honours," to help them ascend towards the light by "a conversion and turning about of the soul from a day whose light is darkness to the veritable day that ascension to reality of our parable which we will affirm to be true philosophy."

Plato examines the sciences with a view to determining "those which lead naturally to pure intelligence." They are related as much to philosophy as to the art of the warrior.

The first to be appropriated is "the science of numbers and calculation,… that naturally conduce to the awakening of thought". Arithmetic (the science of numbers) and logistics (the art of calculation) contain numbers and unity, and "appear to lead to the apprehension of truth", enabling the philosopher to "rise out of the region of generation and lay hold on essence."

The second is geometry, the science of surfaces, which is related to the previous one.

"Then if [geometry] compels the soul to contemplate essence, it is suitable; if genesis, it is not. This at least will not be disputed by those who have even a slight acquaintance with geometry, that this science is in direct contradiction with the language employed in it by its adepts. Their language is most ludicrous, though they cannot help it, for they speak as if they were doing something and as if all their words were directed towards action. For all their talk is of squaring and applying and adding and the like, whereas in fact the real object of the entire study is pure knowledge. That it is the knowledge of that which always is, and not of a something which at some time comes into being and passes away. That is readily admitted, for geometry is the knowledge of the eternally existent. Then, it would tend to draw the soul to truth, and would be productive of a philosophic attitude of mind, directing upward the faculties that now wrongly are turned earthward."

The third is the science which studies "dimension of cubes and of everything that has depth," which will later be called stereometry, and "which has not yet been investigated."

The fourth is astronomy, the science of the movement of solid objects, which enables us to look up, towards being and the invisible things, by using "the blazonry of the heavens as patterns to aid in the study of those realities." Attached to this science of movement is the study of harmony which is not limited to seeking numbers in the harmonies perceived by the ear, but "they do not ascend to generalized problems and the consideration which numbers are inherently concordant and which not and why in each case."

"The investigation of all these studies goes far enough to bring out their community and kinship with one another, and to infer their affinities." "All this procedure of the arts and sciences that we have described indicates their power to lead the best part of

---

[5] All the citations which follow are from Plato, *The Republic*, VII, 517 ff. translated by Paul Shorey (Cambridge MA: Harvard University Press, 1942).

the soul up to the contemplation of what is best among realities."

However, to gain real sight of being other than in a dream, we must abandon the very idea that every hypothesis is intangible, and use dialectics to establish firm conclusions, to reach the intelligible, and to rise up to the principle. For Plato, the synoptic spirit is a dialectician and perceives the relationship, by bringing together that which is scattered, simultaneously, between sciences and being.

The Liberal Arts seem to have been codified later, in the fifth and sixth centuries, inspired by certain doctrines of Pythagoras. In the fifth century, Martianus Capella of Carthage wrote, using literary sources from Greek and Roman antiquity,[6] the *De nuptis Philologiae et Mercurii* in which he seems to have been the first author to set out the whole of the pedagogical framework of the seven liberal arts in a cycle of seven degrees. This text, very well-known and widely circulated from the ninth to the thirteenth centuries, was the touchstone for people of letters.[7] It was taken up and commented on in the ninth century by Remigius (Remigius of Auxerre) and Johannes Scotus Erigena. Translated into old German in the eleventh century by Notker Teutonicus from the monastery of Saint-Gall in Switzerland, the work of Martianus Capella is more famous than those of Boethius[8], Cassiodorus[9], and even the founding text of Isidore of Seville, the *Etymologies*, which was nevertheless quoted in the Cooke manuscript.

On the Marriage of Philology and Mercury[10] presents the seven liberal arts in an allegorical manner in the form of female figures with attributes intended to recall the content of the sciences they personify. Grammar, rhetoric, dialectic, the arts of speech, arithmetic, geometry, astronomy, music, the arts of numbers, physical balance and related subjects, the application of the sciences, using the objects resulting from them, are considered as ways of undertaking inner work, of attaining knowledge. They also reprise a description of the art of memory as a consequence of the teaching of rhetoric.

Martianus Capella excludes medicine and architecture as sciences arising solely from the earthly and material. He does the same for the arts of divination: as they enable mediation with the gods, they stem from a movement descending from the heavens towards the earth. Now, Martianus is heir to Neoplatonism. The soul has "fallen" into matter. For him, science must have the capacity of allowing the heavenly ascent of the soul out of its material vehicle by the means of knowledge in order to attain contemplation of the Intelligible.

Let us return to the details of the text of Martianus Capella, and more specifically to the engagement and marriage of Philology and Mercury in the midst of the assembly of the gods (books I and II). Philology is mortal and in order to wed Mercury, she must attain immortality and ascend to heaven.

---

[6] He drew particular inspiration from Ovid's *Metamorphis* and from *The Golden Ass* or the *Metamorphoses* by Apuleius.

[7] Grégoire de Tours (539¬–594) mentions it in the last chapter of his *Histoire des Francs*. The treaty of Martianus Capella is found in the libraries of Cluny, Rouen, Bayeux, Avignon, Saint-Amand, Corbie and the Sorbonne. Alain de Lille was to take inspiration from it.

[8] *De institutionne arithmetica, De musica, Ars geometrica.*

[9] *De artibus ac disciplinis liberalium litterarum.*

[10] *The Marriage of Philology and Mercury*, translated in *Martianus Capella and the seven Liberal Arts, volume II*, by William Harris Stahl and Richard Johnson with E. L. Burge (New York: Columbia University Press, 1977).

This allegorical tale begins with an invocation: "Sacred principle of unity among the gods, on you I call; you are said to grace weddings with your song; it is said that a Muse was your mother. You bind the warring seeds of the world with secret bonds and encourage the union of opposites by your sacred embrace."

Jupiter describes Mercury as his beloved son, and says of him: "For he is my trust, my speech, my beneficence, and my true genius, the loyal messenger and spokesman of my mind, the sacred 'Nous' (νοῦς).[11] He alone can give the number of the gods, he alone can know the glittering stars, the dimension of the heavens and their depth; he knows the number of the ebb tides, how great are the flood tides the ocean sweeps along its shores[12]; he knows the bond that joins the contrary elements, and I, the father, enforce those bonds through him—perhaps [the goddess] Duty alone will reckon what rewards this obedience will pay." As for Philology, she "penetrates the secrets of knowledge through its patient apprenticeship, and may anticipate everything that it is given to the gods to know it in advance." Jupiter also describes the bride as "the equal [of Mercury] in study," and "she is earthborn, but destined to rise to the stars."

Martianus Capella refers to the use of numerology based on the deconstruction on Greek names into numbers. Thus, the harmony between Philology and Mercury is verified in this way upon their engagement; the name used for this calculation is not the name known by all, nor that given by the peoples, but the secret name of Mercury that Jupiter gave him when he was born, known only to the Egyptians, that is: Thouth (ΘΩΥΘ)[13], of the value of 9+800+400+9, that is 1218, which reduces to 3, a reference to the trivium. The name *Philology*, in Greek, has the value of 724, which reduces to 4, a reference to the quadrivium. "Thus the numbers represented by their names were in concord. Therefore the concord established between them bound their nuptial union with a true proportion."

Philology presents herself for her marriage before the assembly of the gods. Having no doubt of her intellectual ability because of her study and mastery of the seven liberal arts, she will now be able to begin the heavenly ascent which will lead to her deification. However, she fears the passage through the flame of the heavenly spheres, because of "her appearance, her form and her physical substance." She must endure "the fires of burning stars, though her limbs were still those of a mortal." She therefore prepares the unguent of the old man of Abdera [Democritus], based on herbs from Colchis[14,] tufts of grass from Adamantis and green shoots, which will protect her until she is invulnerable to the fires of the

---

[11] Reference to the Neoplatonic concept of the Spirit (νοῦς), considered to be a divine emanation of the Unique One.

[12] We will see later, in the rituals of the Old Charges, that part of the penalties for failure in the oath makes reference to these tides.

[13] *"[Philology] took from each end of his name [Mercury's name] the bonding element that is both the first and perfect terminus of the number. Next came the number which is worshiped as Lord in all temples, for its cubic solidity. In the next position she took a letter which the Samian Sage [Pythagoras] regarded as representing the dual ambiguity of the mortal fate. Accordingly, the number 1218 flashed forth"* (book II, 102).

[14] The herb of Medea.

heavens[15] and the dazzling beauty[16] of the gods. "In the reflection of the moon, she smeared the dewy fluid on her body."[17]

Later, the mother of Philology, Phronesis (Wisdom), clothes her, places a crown on her head and gives her her own belt. Musical instruments play, the assembled choir of the Muses[18] sings, and each of the nine muses addresses the young virgin Philology with sacred words that end: "Ascend into the temples of heaven, maiden, deserving of such a marriage; your father-in-law Jupiter asks you to rise to the lofty stars." Then the virtues—Prudence, Justice, Temperance, and Strength[19]—come into her apartments and show her their face. Philosophy then addresses the fiancée, "proud of the fact that through her Jupiter permitted anyone to ascend to the heavens." Then Philology meets the three Graces (Beauty, Abundance, Joy) who fill her with light.

Finally, Immortality declares to her: "O maiden! the father of the gods has commanded that you be carried to the courts of heaven in this royal palanquin, which no earthborn creature may touch, not even yourself before you drink this cup." She touches her chest, explaining to her "unless you retch violently and void this matter which is choking your breast, you will never attain the throne of immortality at all." Philology vomits, and from her mouth comes forth everything she knows in the form of a torrent of writings in many forms. Immortality, seeing that some were written with sacred ink, has them engraved onto tablets of stone which she places in a cave inside the Egyptian sanctuaries. The Arts and the Disciplines then hasten to collect them for their own use and their particular skills.

Philology then asks for help from Immortality. The latter offers her a cup that she herself received from her own mother, Apotheosis, and says to her: "Drink this so that may be borne up and rise to heaven reinvigorated." She drinks the drink Immortality offers to her in one gulp when she discovers how intensely sweet it is. "And straightway her limbs are strengthened with new vigor, her fragile thinness passes, the power of earth leaves her, and there comes to her the immortality of heaven, free from the laws of death." Philology is then crowned with wild flowers by Immortality and offers sacrificial incense.

Helped by Work, she climbs into the palanquin which Work then carries along with Love, while the rear is borne by Attention and Wakefulness. The whole bridal procession, made up of muses and virtues, accompanies her in her ascension. When she arrives at the summit of the citadel of the heavens, Juno leads her into the heavenly dwellings and shows her the nature

---

[15] Jason uses this same unguent to make himself invulnerable to fire, as does Phoebus when he drives the sun's chariot.

[16] According to Dionysius the Areopagite (fourth century), in the Latin version by John the Saracen of chapter 4 of the *Divine Names* entitled *"The Beautiful and the Good,"* Beauty is the cause of all things that are in harmony (consonantia) and illumination (claritas). *"Beauty is called χαλον as it brings together all separate things into a unique whole." "The beautiful and Beauty are indivisible in their cause, which embraces All in the One."*

[17] The term used by Martianus Capella is *irrorati liquoris,* which refers to the verb *irrorare* meaning to *moisten with dew.*

[18] The muses are daughters of Mnemosyne, Memory.

[19] The cardinal virtues are described in *The Republic* by Plato.

of the various gods and spirits who reign there. After passing through the first interval of the heavenly tones, Philology crosses the circles of the Moon, Mercury and Venus from semi-tone to semi-tone, and then arrives at the fourth circle, that of the Sun, and addresses a prayer to that god, the firstborn of the "Unknown Father who transcends the Universe," entreating him thus: "Hail, true face of the gods, countenance of the Father; your number is 608, and your three letters form the holy name and sign of the Mind.[20] Father of the Mind, allow us to rise up to the heavenly assemblies and come to know the starry sky in the power of your sacred name." She continues her ascension, crosses the dwellings of Mars, Jupiter, and then Saturn. The procession travels around the whole octave in complete and perfect harmony and then rests. Philology descends from her palanquin, sees the light, finds celestial peace, and contemplates the cosmos that the Unknown Father has organized in the reality of pure comprehension.[21] She prays silently, invoking inwardly the names of certain gods. "With these prayers she long besought with her whole heart the flower of the fire and that truth which arises from nonexistent things (the uncreated truth); then she seemed to perceive that she had earned deification and worship." In the Milky Way, Jupiter and the assembly of the gods await her, and they invite Philology together with the Muses and her mother, Wisdom, to draw near. The marriage with Mercury is then celebrated.

Phoebus brings seven sisters belonging to the house of Mercury, radiant with beauty. These seven sciences, which in the Middle Ages will make up the trivium and the quadrivium, express themselves one after the other and develop their teaching.

The description of the Liberal Arts given by Martianus Capella is as follows:

- *Grammar*, also called Literature by Romulus, carries a medicine case comprising a "pruning knife", a file with eight divisions, a whip, and tools for treating the vices of language, ink, pens, writing tablets.

- *Dialectics*, with artfully rolled hair, carries in her left hand a snake which is half hidden by her dress, and in her right hand she holds a wax tablet and a hook.

- *Rhetoric* is a virgin wearing a helmet, bearing weapons gleaming like lightning. Martianus Capella describes her as the "Excellence and exaltation of speech, genius of argumentation, abundance and richness of diction, vast store of memory and recollection." The art of memory, which is an integral part of rhetoric, "must be exercised on distinct topics, to which should be attributed material forms and representations of ideas." "The memory of things is contained in images as if in letters." "Then it will be of advantage to make symbols individually at those points which we particularly want to remember; they should not be read out loud, but rather memorized in our hearts."

- *Geometry*, clothed in a dress embroidered with the movements of the stars, carries an armillary sphere (a model of the objects in the sky) in her left hand and a compass

---

[20] The Greek word ϕρη (phre), with the value 608, designates an Eqyptian sun god, and is close to ϕρην (phren) meaning mind, spirit.

[21] Philology travels through the nine zones of the universe: "*The earthly sphere, the seven belonging to the gods, and the celestial sphere.*" This configuration is found in the Jewish mystic formulation of the Merkabah and in Christian angelology.

(radius) in her right hand. In front of her there is an abacus on which she is drawing diagrams. At the end of her demonstration, she teaches Euclid's first proposition, that is, the construction of an equilateral triangle upon a given finite straight line.

- *Arithmetic* comes next, escorted by Pythagoras holding a lighted torch. From her forehead beams a ray of light from which the first decade emerges, then an infinite number of rays which finally reduce themselves to one, Unity. "Arithmetic, by way of greeting Jupiter, made a finger calculation[22], expressed the numbers seven hundred, ten, and seven", "the very own name of Jupiter." Remigius of Auxerre would explain the harmony of this number with the letters of the Greek name of Jupiter, H APXH (The Beginning, The Principle), equivalent to the sum of the numbers 8+1+100+600+8. In ancient Greek arithmetical treatises, this mystical treatment of numbers is called arithmology.

- *Astronomy* is shining with heavenly light and crowned with stars, carrying in one hand a sextant and in the other a book made of several metals containing the calculations of the movements of the planets and constellations.

- *Harmony* [Music] finally comes forward accompanied by gods, goddesses, poets and musicians, dressed in a garment with incised and laminated gold which tinkle with every measured step and movement of her body. In one hand she carries musical instruments of the theatre, and in the other a round gold shield made of concentric circles that resound in harmony with each other, and give out inexpressible melodies "which were pouring forth in honor of a certain secret fire and inextinguishable flame, reverenced the profound ancestral song, and one by one arose in homage to extramundane intelligence."

————————

From the sixth century, the liberal arts were organized in three and four series. The first three formed the trivium,[23] disciplines of speech, the science of letters, and the next four formed the quadrivium,[24] mathematical arts, the science of numbers.

The teaching of the seven liberal arts, taken directly from the work of Martianus Capella, spread through many schools, in particular those of Laon, Auxerre, and Chartres. The latter made links between the philosophy of Plato and Pythagoras, and Christianity. The masters of this school, such as Thierry de Chartres (+1155) and Jean de Salisbury (1115–1180), wrote the *Heptateuchon*, a treatise on the seven liberal arts, and the *Metalogicon*, on the study of the trivium, respectively.

Medieval sculptors reproduced the imagery of the seven liberal arts according to the ancient model on the royal doorway

---

[22] Certain numbers are counted on the fingers of both hands, but "in other cases, we must resort to contorted movements of the arms in order to make numbers correspond to the figures and lines dealt with by my sister [Geometry] who discoursed before me."

[23] The first appearance of the term *trivium* is in the *Scholia Vindobonensia ad Horatii Artem poeticam*, a text that could go back to the eighth or ninth century, known by one single manuscript which dates from the eleventh century.

[24] The term *quadrivium* seems to have been used for the first time by Boethius in his *Institution arithmétique*, I, 1, 7, written at the beginning of the sixth century: "This is the quadruple path by which all those must walk whose superior spirit allows itself to be led by the senses created with us to the highest certainties of intelligence" (French transl. Jean-Yves Guillaumin (Paris: Les Belles Lettres, 1995)).

into Chartres cathedral, on the façade and rose window of the north transept of Laon cathedral,[25] on the west façade of Auxerre cathedral, as well as at Sens, Soissons, Rouen, Clermont, Paris, and Fribourg in Brisgau.[26] However, Music differs from the representation given by Martianus Capella: she appears in the form of a seated woman striking three or four bells with hammers, recalling the myth of Tubal inventing music by striking a hammer. Whereas Vincent de Beauvais declared in his *Miroir doctrinal* that "man can rise up from his fall by science" and sees this only from the perspective of his salvation, other authors envisage that man can attain the heavenly spaces, right up to the throne of God, and be deified. The seven liberal arts make up a ladder leading to Philosophy, an open door to knowledge of God. That is why on certain cathedrals Philosophy[27] (Wisdom) is shown carrying two books, one open and the other closed, a scepter, and the ladder that must be climbed to reach Knowledge and ultimate sight.

Knowledge of the liberal arts was not restricted solely to the clerics, who were its guardians in the eleventh and twelfth centuries: in the Middle Ages they spread it very widely among working people and the general population in France, England, Germany, and Italy. *The Drama of Paphnutius*, a mystery play dating from the tenth century, was written by Hrotswithe, a Benedictine nun from the abbey of Gandersheim in Germany, and features the hermit Paphnutius, his disciples, and Thaïs the courtesan in the Egyptian desert. It contains a long dialogue on the liberal arts and in particular on music and its relationship to the heavenly spheres. The quadrivium is defined thus: "The straight lines of these four sciences start out from the single principle of philosophy, just like the roads at a crossroads."[28] The drama ends with the conversion of Thaïs, her seclusion in a monastic cell, and her death.

The liberal arts were known and practiced in the world of the Jews in the twelfth century. Rabbi Abraham ben Meir ibn Ezra was a medieval poet, mathematician, astrologer, grammarian, and philosopher. He was born in 1092 in Toledo, and moved to Cordoba. From 1140, he travelled to Rome, Lucca, Mantua, Verona, Narbonne, and Béziers, where he wrote a work, the *Sefer haShem*, dealing with holy names and the numbers associated with them. He then went to Dreux and Rouen, and in 1158 to London and Oxford. In 1160, he returned to Narbonne and translated an astronomical treatise from Arabic. He died around 1164, probably in Rome.

Considered one of the most eminent rabbinical authorities of the medieval age, he wrote a book, *The Foundation of Awe and the Secret of the Torah*, in which the first chapter deals with the different branches of knowledge: "Each branch of knowledge gives life to the one who acquires it. . . . However, only when someone knows the natural sciences and their proofs does he learn the categories which are the 'guardians of the walls (of reason),' taught

---

[25] The representation of the Liberal Arts and wisdom was commissioned by Gautier de Mortagne, Bishop of Laon, and schoolmaster in the same town.

[26] See the detail of this iconography in Émile Mâle, *L'art religieux du XIIIe siècle en France*, Volume I, Book 2, *Le Miroir de la science* (Paris: Armand Colin, 1910).

[27] The following description is in accordance with the vision of Boethius, *The Consolation of Philosophy*, trans. Victor Watts (London: Penguin Books, 1999), Book I, Chap. 1.

[28] The Count of Douhet, *Dictionnaire des mystères* (Paris: J.-P. Migne, 1854).

by the science of logic, by the masters of the science of astronomy, with its absolute proofs, based on mathematical knowledge, and comprehends the sciences of geometry and proportions, can one ascend to the great level of knowing the secret of the soul, the secret of the supernal angels, and the concept of the world to come (as taught in) the Torah, the Prophets, and by the sages of the Talmud. Such an individual will grasp and perceive the deep secrets, a few of which I shall explain, that are hidden from the eyes of most people."

Ibn Ezra also wrote an allegorical story in rhyming prose, entitled *Hayy ben Meqitz*, in which an old man leads the narrator towards wisdom, making him drink spiced wine and the waters of the fountain of life, which allows him to accomplish the ascension through the heavenly spheres, to contemplate the reality of the angels, and, if he agrees to follow in his guide's footsteps, to attain the knowledge and sight of "the One who has no second."

————————

The liberal arts are only rarely mentioned in the statutes of the Communities of professions (Corporations) in France. They are found in the statutes of locksmiths of 1650.[29] Article 12 mentions them to justify removing 'lettres de maîtrise', sometimes sold to master workers of poor quality: "And in order for the art of these so-called masters to be happily preserved in the splendor it has always merited, both because of its necessity as well as for the rare inventions it produces, even considering that it is one of the four liberal arts

whose recommendation is so very dear to Us. . . . We have from now on removed and revoked all letters of the said art, conceded in favor of births, marriages, sacraments, coronations, entrances into our towns, and in general for all other occasions whatsoever."

The Liberal Arts were not only practiced by the building professions. We can quote this anecdote from an extract from the Reception of hunters in Germany around 1700:

> - Good hunter, tell me why is the hunter called a master hunter?
> - A skillful hunter, sure of his aim, obtains from princes and lords the favor of being called master in the seven liberal arts (Freien Kunst).[30]

————————

Let us now return to the Liberal Arts described in the Old Charges of the English masons and to their mythical origins. The first known text which mentions them is the Regius manuscript, a poem dating from 1390: "This honest craft of good masonry was ordained and made in this manner, counterfeited of these clerks together; at these lord's prayers they counterfeited geometry, and gave it the name of masonry, for the most honest craft of all."

"Many years after, the good clerk Euclid taught the craft of geometry full wonder wide, so he did that other time also, of divers crafts many more. Through high grace of Christ in heaven, he commenced in the sciences seven; Grammar is the first science I know, Dialect the second, so I have

---

[29] Statutes of the locksmiths in 68 articles, reformed by Louis XIV (under the Regency of Anne of Austria), dating from October 12, 1650 and recorded at Parliament on January 27, 1652. Cited by François Husson, *Les serruriers, étude historique* (Paris: Marchal et Billard, 1902).

[30] Jacob Grimm, *Altdeutsche Wœlder* (Kassel, Germany: Thurniessen 1816), 112, taken up by Jules Michelet, *Introduction à l'Histoire Universelle* (Paris: Hachette, 1834), 135 ff.

I bliss, Rhetoric the third without doubt, Music is the fourth, as I you say, Astronomy is the fifth, by my snout, Arithmetic the sixth, without doubt, Geometry the seventh maketh an end."

Not only masons, but also other professions needed to know them: "Merchants and all Craftsmen, and others who use the seven Sciences, and especially the ploughmen and tillers of all types of grains and seeds, the planters of vineyards and setters of other fruit: for none can act without Geometry; neither in Grammar, Rhetoric, or Astronomy, nor in any of the others, can any man find length or measure without Geometry. So I think this Science may well be called the most worthy Science, for it is the foundation of all others."[31] This text was to be taken up with a few variations in various English and Scottish manuscripts and publications from 1550 to 1750,[32] then gradually disappeared from the writings of Masonry known as Speculative.

In these same documents, definitions of the liberal arts appear in the following manner:

Grammar teaches Man "to speak rightfully and to write truly."

Rhetoric. The anonymous Roman Master of rhetoric who wrote *Ad Herennium* in 86–82 BC describes the five parts of Rhetoric as follows: inventio, dispositio, elocutio, memoria, pronuntiatio. "It measureth with ornate speech among," Regius Ms. (1390). "It teaches us to speak formally and fair," Cooke Ms. (1410), "in subtle terms," Grand Lodge Ms. (1583).

Dialectics (also called Logic) "teaches one to discern and recognize the true from the false." The Henery Head (1675) and Watson Mss. (1687) call them the *Art of Sophistry*. Called Philosophy in the Thistle Ms. (1756), it is defined by the love "of wisdom by which is brought both ends of a contradiction together and crocked things made straight black grouen white by a Rule of contrarities, etc."[33] It is the practice of antinomy.[34]

Arithmetic "sheweth one thing that is [equal] another," Regius Ms. (1390). The other Old Charges say that it "teaches a man to reckon and count all manners of numbers."

Geometry, the fifth science, "teaches a man boundaries and measures and computations or weights of all manner of Crafts." Gemetria means "the measure of the earth," Cooke Ms. (1410). In the Wood Ms. (1610),

[31] Grand Lodge Ms. No. 1, 1583.
[32] Mss. Watson (1687), Dowland (1550–1815), Grand Lodge No. 1 (1583), York No. 1 (1600), Thorp (1629), Grand Lodge (1632), Sloane No. 3848 (1646), Taylor (1650–1700), Harleian No. 2054 (1650–1700), Sloane No. 3323 (1659), Edinburg-Kilwinning (1675–1678), Harleian No. 1942 (1650–1700), Dumfries No. 1 and No. 3 (c. 1650–1700), Henery Head (1675), Hope (1650–1700), Buchanan (c. 1670), Antiquity (1686), York No. 4 (1693), Rawlinson (1700–1750), Thomas Tew (1700–1750), Alnwick (1701), Dumfries No. 4 (1710), Papworth (1750–1800), Maknab (1722), Briscoe (1724), Cole (1728), Fortitude (c. 1750), Harris (c. 1750–1800). The manuscripts and publications of the Spencer Family (Mss. Inigo Jones (c. 1655–1725), Fisher-Rosedale (c. 1726), Songhurst (c. 1726), Spencer (1726), Cole (1729) and Dodd (1739)) offer a variation: "That every Crafts man works by Measure. He buys or sells, is by weight or Measure. Husbandmen, Navigators, Planters and all of them use Geometry; for neither Grammar, Logick nor any other of the said Sciences, can subsist without Geometry; ergo, most Worthy and Honourable."
[33] Dumfries Ms. No. 4 (1710).
[34] We understand that Dialectics here has little to do with dialectics as it was understood from the eighteenth century to today. These two conceptions arise from modes of expression or rather structures of thought that are very distinct. The first functions according to an antinomic approach in which the real is expressed both by a thing and by its opposite, considered simultaneously and representative of the "real" whereas the second is based on reasoning in which oppositions are resolved by synthesis.

this science is also called "Masonry."[35] Allied to arithmetic, the science of numbers, it presides over the art of construction, both exterior and interior. Geometry is at the center of the activities of medieval masons.[36]

Music is a "sweet song," Regius Ms. (1390), it teaches "the Craft of song and voice of tongue, organ, harp and trumpet," Cooke Ms. (1410) and Grand Lodge Ms. (1583), "the art of composition," Inigo Jones Ms. (c. 1655–1725), and was invented by Jubal or Tubal "by the sound of ponderation of his brother's hammers, that was Tubal Cain," Cooke Ms. (1410). It teaches harmonious relationships between numbers giving access to the music of the heavenly spheres.

Music therefore teaches the numeric relationships of intervals, the relation of numbers between themselves, and the proportions based on arithmetic, the whole a direct product of the science of Pythagoras. Numbers and sounds correspond to names and words in a similar way to the transcendent order of the universe, introducing the harmony of the macrocosm.[37] Musical relationships also make it possible to calculate architectural proportions,[38] the earthly reflections of the music of the heavenly spheres.

Astronomy "numbereth," Regius Ms. (1390). To all the other Old Charges, it "teaches the course of the sun, and the moon and the other stars and planets in the sky," and the "ornaments of the heavens," according to the Sloane No. 3848 (1646)

and Taylor Mss. (1650–1700). Knowledge of it enables one, among other things, to calculate the comput (the calculation of the movable feasts in the calendar), and determine the siting of a building for its foundations as well as being used in the construction of buildings.

In medieval thinking, there is a relationship between the arts and the seven planetary heavens, and the ascension which results from climbing their ladder recalls the paths to the internal realization of certain gnoses and of the Judaic system of the Merkabah. Seeing the persistence of medieval representations of the Four Living Creatures (Man, Lion, Bull, Eagle), we may well wonder if speculations relating to the Chariot of God as it is described in the vision of Ezekiel[39] and the practices of heavenly ascension in relationship with the art of memory may not have influenced the stone mason Companions and the *ymagiers*[40] in their iconographic representations.

Medieval laborers were not the uneducated workmen that the nineteenth century, preoccupied largely by social progress, wished to present to us. Deeply rooted in a society steeped in religiosity and marked by the omnipresence of the image and the symbol, they were concerned with the perfection of their work, the acquisition of the virtues associated with it, and the spiritual elevation of their being. To accomplish this work it was necessary to practice the profession, and to be aware of the simultaneity of external and internal realization.

---

[35] The Harris Ms. (c. 1750–1800) differs from the other Old Charges, and calls this science "*Free Masonrie.*"

[36] Speculative masonry still gives it a place of prime importance, but totally ignores its content and the metaphysical applications which result from it. The 1723 constitutions retain it as a foundation.

[37] See on this subject the article by Jacques Viret, Institut de Musicologie de Strasbourg, "L'enseignement musical au Moyen Âge," *Chant Floral* 45 (1985).

[38] In the fifteenth century, the architect Léon-Battista Alberti wrote the *De re aedificatoria* (1485), in which he proposed the relationship between architectural proportions and the numbers linked to musical intervals.

[39] Chapters 1 and 2.

[40] This term designates the painters-glassmakers and the carvers of images in the sense of statues.

The Stuarts and Freemasonry: The Final Episode

Pierre Mollier[A]

The connection between the Stuarts and Freemasonry remains one of the key elements in the Masonic imagination of the eighteenth century. Many rituals or correspondence documents explain that since time immemorial, the Stuarts were the protectors and secret leaders of the Order. Some even add that the Lodges had a hidden goal to reinstate the unfortunate Scottish dynasty to their legitimate place on the throne. Perhaps there is no smoke without fire, but historians today can still find no documented testimonies on the real involvement of the "pretenders" into Freemasonry. Rare elements emerge, such as the attested existence of a "Jacobite" Lodge in Rome in James III of England's entourage, or that of a few manifestly Stuartist Lodges identified in Paris in the 1730s by Pierre Chevallier. However, conversely, all the patents or charters supposedly granted, signed, or promulgated by the Stuarts have proven to be false. Before looking deeper into the matter, it is useful to retrace the history of the legend.

From 1653, the Perth Lodge exhibited a parchment asserting that James VI of Scotland was received as an Entered Apprentice on April 15, 1601. From 1737, there were rumors among Parisian Masons about the

existence of a Lodge during the exile (from 1688) in Saint-Germain-en-Laye. In 1749, the ritual of the Sublime Order of Knights Elect asserted that the pursued Templars were welcomed and protected by the Stuart Kings in Scotland, where they hid in Masonic Lodges. The legend thrived even more thanks to the strong romantic dimension it gained from the personality, saga, and tragic fate of Bonnie Prince Charlie—Charles Edward Stuart, known as the "young pretender" (1720–1788). I would like to take this opportunity to relate a later but very real episode, in which the last Stuart became involved in Freemasonry[1] to (finally!) take on the role of secret Grand Master that everyone credited him with.

I. 1777: "Successor to My Ancestors in Masonry"

Probably from the 1740s, and certainly in 1749, the Sublime Order of Knights Elect asserted that modern Freemasonry came from the Templars who escaped persecution at the hands of Philippe le Bel (Philip IV of France) and took refuge in Scotland under the protection of the Stuart Kings. The three ingredients of this "Templar

---

[A] Director of the Grand Orient de France Library and of the Museum of Freemasonry (Paris).
[1] My attention was brought to this matter by a note from my friend Pierre Noël in "Réaction à la conférence 'Un rituel inédit de langue française, daté de 1758,'"*Acta Macionica* 11 (2001): 359–360. Noël points out and refers to the published work that contains some of the documents relating to Charles Edward's declarations on Freemasonry during his exile in Florence: Pericle Maruzzi, *La Stretta Osservanza Templare e il Regime Scozzese Rettificato in Italia nel secolo XVIII* (Rome: Atanòr, 1990).

doi: 10.18278/rscs.3.1.3

legend" (the Order of the Temple, Scotland, and the Stuarts) are seen in many of the High Chivalric Degrees, which expanded from 1750. Given the dynamism of the Lodges in the eighteenth century, including in the high aristocracy of the European courts, the question of their real connections with Freemasonry was necessarily asked of the Stuarts themselves by some of their eminent interlocutors. In his meeting with Baron de Waechter, Charles Edward confirmed that he discussed Freemasonry with his father "on several occasions."

Whether calculatingly (as in the accusations of modern critics) or in good faith as I believe, Baron von Hund, "Eques ab Ense i.o.," preserved this Templar and Stuartist genealogy when he began developing the "Strict Templar Observance" in Germany from 1750. He claimed that he had been received in Paris in the 1740s, into the restored Order of the Temple, within a Lodge bringing together English and Scottish members of the entourage of Charles Edward Stuart, the "young pretender." He was led to believe that Charles Edward was the secret Grand Master of the Masons, under the name "Eques a Sole Aureo." The Freemasonry that concealed the secret continuation of the Order of the Temple was in reality led by "Unknown Superiors." He was finally entrusted with the restoration of the "Seventh Province," between the Elbe and the Oder, of the Order of the Temple. From 1770, the Order became increasingly successful. However, at the same time, its founder gradually lost his influence, while that of dignitaries of a higher social rank increased. Thus, after his death on October 28, 1776, the leadership of the Order fell into the hands of two rival princes:

Ferdinand, Duke of Brunswick-Lüneburg, "Eques a Victoria i.o.," and Charles, Duke of Sudermania, "Eques a Sole Vivificante i.o." and brother of King Gustav III of Sweden, himself "Eques a Corona Vindicata i.o." They were significant figures in Europe during the 1770s and 1780s, which helps to explain the three events that I am about to recount.

The nagging question of the origins of the Order and the somewhat muddled explanations from its founder, Baron von Hund, perturbed and divided several Convents of the Strict Observance. In 1777, shortly after becoming Magnus Magister Ordinis, Ferdinand of Brunswick sent a very active Mason, Baron de Waechter—Eques a Ceraso—to the "young pretender," (who in fact was no longer young), to (finally!) interrogate him "officially" on the real connections between the Stuarts and Freemasonry.

That Charles Edward[2] participated with good grace was clearly owing to the eminent rank of the duke who sent Waechter, but also undoubtedly because he was in a very difficult situation at the time. The days when Europe was passionate about the Stuartist cause—when they had great support from continental monarchies, and when the exploits of 1745 were fresh in everyone's minds—had long passed. In that year, Bonnie Prince Charlie (who was barely twenty-five years old) had arrived in Scotland and narrowly missed regaining his throne with the support of his Highlanders. This saga had kept the whole of Europe on the edge of its seat. Thirty years on, everyone had long stopped believing that the Stuarts would return, and the major states had finally normalized their relations with Hanoverian England. At fifty-seven years old, Charles

---

[2] On the life of Charles Edward Stuart, it is useful to consult Michel Duchein's *Les derniers Stuarts 1660–1807* (Paris: Fayard, 2006), particularly chapter 13, "La Fin des Stuarts 1744–1807," on the end of the Stuarts. Also useful is the reference biography published by Frank McLynn, *Charles Edward Stuart: A Tragedy in Many Acts* (London: Routledge, 1988).

Edward was a man broken by political and personal failures and diminished by alcohol. It was all he could do to welcome the eminent people who took an interest in him, even if they did so for unusual reasons.

Waechter was a lawyer, and he left a precise account of his meeting with Charles Edward, who at the time was hiding (without really fooling anyone) behind the title of the Count of Albany. The text[3] is fascinating, and I would like to offer readers a full reproduction of this very lively account:

The Privy Counsellor of Waechter's Legation for the Duke of Saxe-Gotha, having been a deputy in the united lodges of Germany and of the Neighboring States, asked the Count of Albany whether he had been told by his late Father that the Dignity of Grand Master of the Freemasons had been hereditary in the illustrious House of the Stuarts since King Charles II of Great Britain, whether he had consequently received the related Papers & Documents, whether he wished to transmit them to the united Lodges, thereby legitimating himself as the Grand Master & Leader, & being recognized by those in this eminent Charge to their reciprocal benefits;

The said Privy Counsellor of Waechter's Legations requested that the Count tell him the day & time when he might have the honor of discussing with him the important subject of his Commission; the Count did this, giving him this day, and he discharged his Commission by informing the Count of the intentions of the united Lodges, & requesting that he answer honestly, as could be expected of a man of universally recognized probity,

& trusting his honor concerning the absolute silence that the importance of the affair required from both Parties.

The Count was kind enough to answer this proposal by saying that he had not been informed at all of anything that might be connected with Masonry, that, given that several illustrious men of his House had been Masons, he had several times indicated to his late Father his desire to become one, but that his father had always opposed this; that his late father had told him several times that he was not a Mason, that he had therefore not given to him any Paper on the matter, and that if he had been so himself, his extreme devotion would certainly have led him to renounce Masonry after the late Pope Benedict XIV's Bull condemning it; that he possessed many Papers belonging to his late Father and kept in Rome, but that he was sure they could contain nothing of interest, because his brother had assured him of this, after examining them.

That his late father had left him two more Crates full of Papers, but that these were sealed in St. Germain en Laye, & that he had so far not expected any certain chance to send for them, although he believed that the crate he had not yet opened contained nothing relating to Masonry. He declared his intention to do this immediately, & stated that he was consequently very disposed to contribute in any way to the Objectives that the united Lodges might have, but he was only obliged to declare in advance that he could spend nothing in this whole affair, & to beg that the Privy Counsellor of

---

[3] Transcribed and published in Maruzzi, *La Stretta Osservanza Templare*, 96–98.

Waechter's Legation agree a Figure with him to reciprocally communicate useful News.

The Count answered two other questions from the Privy Counsellor of Waechter's Legation: whether a certain Lord Sackville had been connected to his late Father & whether the Count had had in his service, several years ago, a certain Giacomo Approsi? That he had never known the former, that Lord Guérit had been his last secretary, & that he had not been in his service for three years, and that he took take of his affairs himself.

The Privy Counsellor of Waechter's Legation then asked the Count to give him permission to produce an Extract of their Interview, to make two copies of it, & to leave one with the Count, & use the other to give himself legitimacy with the Masonic Superiors, the Count gave his permission readily, also making a solemn promise to maintain perfect silence about [this] whole affair, & upon receiving that of the said Privy Counsellor of Waechter's Legation, to only give Report of it to the Masonic Superiors.

The Count, in witness of the above, put his seal on a Copy & received from the Privy Counsellor of Waechter's Legation another, also signed and sealed with his mark.

Written in Florence, September 21 of the Year 1777.

Note.

All of this was written in the Count of Albany's own hand:

Nothing in the world could flatter me more & I would consider it a very great honor if I were to be recognized as successor to my ancestors in Masonry

Florence, September 21, 1777
[signed] Count of Albany

Charles Edward's answers were sincere, but of course deceptive for adepts of the Templar and Jacobite origins of Masonry. However, the last phrase left a mixed impression, and these due confessions would not definitively close the debate. By attributing the origins and leadership of the Order to "Unknown Superiors" whose mystery masked the significance, Baron von Hund had, undoubtedly involuntarily, invented a formidable concept. Charles Edward's denials and his uncomfortable response do not in any way prove he was not the Unknown Superior. After all, by definition, did such superiors not have to do everything they could to conceal their status and mission? Moreover, as a repercussion of the failure of 1745 and his shady and unpredictable character, from 1750 and until his father died in 1766, Charles Edward led a rather mysterious life: for no real reason, he disappeared. He became anonymous: hidden behind various pseudonyms and an unremarkable appearance, he traveled Europe unbeknown to everyone, even those closest to him. Nobody knew where he was. Of course, from time to time, he was recognized, but a few days later, he would disappear again and nobody would hear of him for months, until a police force traced him in another town. It was an astonishing way of life, which in combination with his well-known taste for secrecy and dissimulation[4] made the idea of an "Unknown Superior" on a secret mission credi-

---

[4] As emphasized by his biographer Frank McLynn in *Charles Edward Stuart*, 533.

ble. Still, contact was maintained. Waechter wrote to him regularly to obtain information on various details of the history of the Stuarts and their partisans that might potentially reveal connections with Freemasonry.[5] German Masons also showed great interest in the papers of James II kept in Saint-Germain-en-Laye, but Charles Edward ignored them. Waechter even sent an emissary to Florence to try and get them. He was turned away, and when Waechter was surprised by this, Charles Edward answered that since the emissary had not introduced himself as a representative of the Masons, he had feared it was a trap!

II. 1780: The First Swedish Attempt

Under the direction of Baron von Hund, the "Seventh Province" of the Strict Templar Observance had been the cradle for the modern renaissance of the Order. Hund's disappearance in 1776 marked the start of a period of intense negotiations for the succession of Eques ab Ense. After three years, in spite of major reservations on the part of Ferdinand of Brunswick, who was hardly pleased to see an important figure counteracting his authority at the head of the Order, the Duke of Sudermania was finally named Grand Master of the Seventh Province. Whether he was not familiar with the "Waechter Report," or whether he did not believe it, several weeks after beginning his new functions, on December 11, 1779, he decided to inform Charles Edward. It is true that in Stockholm, the Master of Ceremonies of the Court, Brother von Plommenfeldt, was a firm believer in the Jacobite affilia-

tion and claimed to have received proof of it from Charles Edward himself during a trip to Florence. On January 18, 1780, Duke Charles wrote the following letter to the "pretender."[6]

The first duty of every man of honor is to try and be able, with the Help of the very high, to meet the Commitments he has made, & to try in his behavior to merit the Esteem of those who Are above him & the Trust of those who must obey him, I am currently performing one of these duties, & performing it with even greater Pleasure because in doing so, I hope to be able to establish a close Liaison with a Prince famous for both his Virtues and his misfortunes, whom I have always held in infinite esteem. Having been elected Leader of the Seventh Province, it is my duty to pay the tribute I owe to my Leader to the Grand Master of our Holy Order. By the sublime Theoretical Wisdom entrusted to me by Brother von Plommenfeldt in the Knightly Order known as Stella immaculata & in the Sanctuary known under the Name of Bias, which he brought from Florence, I learned to know my Grand Master & the Grand Master of the whole Holy Order, who I had long desired to know; but let him not himself refuse me the Certainty I have just received from his Person, & let him be Good enough to ratify with an Act of his hand, the Choice that the Seventh Province has just made. The Laws that have been entrusted to me order that all the Leaders of Provinces must be named or approved by the Grand Master, & I am the first to desire that this Law be applied to me.

---

[5] Elements reported by Frank McLynn based on the "Stuart Papers" kept at Windsor, in McLynn, *Charles Edward Stuart*, 534.

[6] Working documents of the Convent of Wilhelmsbad, Library of the Grand Orient de France, donated by Alain Bauer, AR.

Very enlightened, very Illustrious, & very worthy Brother, if you grant me Your suffrage, allow me to report to you the detail of the Province & give me Your orders by Consequence, I will look upon You as a Father, consider myself a son who, enlightened by Your Advice, will take double pleasure in fulfilling Commitments made out of pure Zeal for the Holy Order at the Feet of its altars & of which the sincere objective is to persevere to the detriment of all else, to reach A close liaison with these tender Fathers who made a spark of the true Light shine in out Northern Climates. Convinced that my pleas will not be refused & that You will not turn away a Child who has so long sought his Father without success, & who hopes in finding him to find within himself the aim & the recompense for all the works. If I am permitted this hope, my Gratitude will be eternal & will increase my strength so that I can acquire the Qualities to deserve the Trust that I dare to request. But if my Wishes are not heeded, I will content myself in my Grief with the little that I know, I will arm myself with the Patience of Job, & I will await with Resignation the right moment when he Wishes to look upon me. I will however have fulfilled my duty, & I will inside myself restrict myself to making the ardent Vows I must make to earn the Trust of my Superior & of my Leader. It is with these sentiments that I recommend myself, very enlightened, very Illustrious, & very worthy Brother in Your tender friendship, with the highest Respect, & inviolable Affection.

Very enlightened, very Illustrious, & very worthy Brother,
Stockholm, January 18, 1780.
Your affectionate & devoted Brother
Carolus a Sole vivificante Dux Sud

To this eloquent and lengthy missive, the "Count of Albany" gave a very cordial reply—though one that was also belated, short, and rather disappointing:

> *My eternal affection and gratitude for the very obliging Letter that H.R.H. kindly wrote to me through Mr. Borguinstierna. The New Degree that he has just received could not have fallen into better Hands.*
>
> *The total Darkness in which I reside concerning the Mysteries prevents me from saying anything further, until I am Enlightened. I beg HRH to be persuaded of my respect & the sincere affection I will always have for Him and his august Family.*
>
> *The C. of Al. Sept 25, 1780.*

But once again, this admission of ignorance from the pretender, as clear as it may be, only convinced those who wanted to be convinced. Was his awkwardness in itself not suspicious? The formidable notion of the Unknown Superior once more provided an explanation for these uncomfortable denials: the duty of secrecy. It is worth noting that the Duke of Sudermania did envisage this hypothesis at the end of his letter, in which he announces his patient resignation if his request is not granted.

III. 1783: An Authentic Jacobite Masonic Patent

The Swedish, fervent believers in the Jacobite filiation, made a third attempt. This would be a success. It is possible that the apparent credulity of the Stockholm dignitaries also hid various political agendas. An authentic document from the Stuart pretender was a major advantage with regard to Masonic figures in their rivalry with Ferdinand von Brunswick. More-over, Gustav III had in mind a claim to Li-vonia, which in the Middle Ages was under the rule of the Teutonic Order. A title on the Order of the Temple—assimilated on this occasion with the Teutonics—could provide an additional argument. The fact remains that, during a visit to Italy, the King of Swe-den made the pilgrimage to Florence. In De-cember 1783,[7] Gustav III accompanied by his friend and favorite Armfelt, whose father had participated in the Forty-Five, visited Charles Edward and had several discussions with him.[8] He was profoundly moved by the distress of James II's grandson,[9] who was ag-ing, abandoned by his young wife, penniless, and without support. The "young pretender," now a slightly senile old man who struggled to walk, told him the same anecdotes sever-al times. The King of Sweden wrote to Louis XVI and to the King of Spain to obtain assis-tance for him, and also granted him an an-nual pension of five hundred pounds from his personal treasury. Shortly afterwards, in Rome, he arranged with the Holy See under the best conditions his separation from the Countess of Albany. It was at this time that, out of gratitude, Charles Edward granted the title he so desired. But beyond the different services that he received from Gustav III, Charles Edward was above all struck by the fact that the King of a European power, for the first time in so long, had come to see him

ex officio, and treated him respectfully, as an equal. This was in contrast to the Grand Duke of Tuscany, who in ten years had not deigned to travel five hundred meters to come and see him.

Thus, for the first time, the only au-thentic Jacobite Masonic patent is revealed:

We Charles Edward[10]

By the grace of God Sovereign Lead-er and Hereditary Grand Master of the Holy Order of the Knights of Saint John of the Temple of our Lord Jesus Christ, last Prince and legitimate Heir of the Royal House of the Stuarts, to all our dear and respectable brothers who will read these patent letters, Salutations.

Considering that we have no children, that the life of man is in the hands of God, his eternal wisdom can prolong it for more long years as well as cutting it short and ending it when we least expect it, and that by the laws of this Holy Or-der, of which the Supreme Government and the hereditary Grand Mastery have been passed down to us by the Kings our Ancestors and our Predecessors, we are obliged not to let this Eminent Dignity die out in our person, who as the last of the Royal House of the Stuarts possesses it; we have taken it upon ourselves to choose

---

[7] There is some doubt concerning the exact date of the meeting. Claude Nordmann (see below), uses the Swedish royal archives to date it to December 21, 1783, but the patent signed by Charles Edward (of which we only possess a copy and not the original, possibly incorrect on this matter: 8 for 28?) is dated December 8.

[8] René Leforestier, *La Franc-Maçonnerie Occultiste et Templière aux XVIIIe et XIXe siècles*, 2 vols. (Paris: La Table d'Emeraude, 1987); this second edition published by Antoine Faivre includes addenda and an index. The author briefly relates the episode in a note (2:698n54). He indicates that the English diplomatic archives retain traces of these meetings in the reports sent to London by Sir Horace Mann, British ambassador in Florence, whose informer, it seems, was the same Chevalier des Tours who organized the meeting.

[9] These elements are taken from: Claude Nordmann, *Gustave III, un démocrate couronné* (Lille: Presses Uni-versitaires de Lille, 1986), 219.

[10] Facsimile of the French copy of the patent, private collection. My warmest thanks go to my dear Brother and friend S. for having made this extremely rare document available to me.

and elect a Successor and a Coadjutor in hereditary Grand Mastery of the Order, who after our death can succeed us in governing it, which following this choice must always remain under the direction of a supreme Leader, who can at the same time protect it and maintain its laws in their purity.

Then considering that this Dignity must always be exercised by a crowned head, as it was conferred by the unanimous votes of the whole Order to the first King of our House who held it and from whom we have received it, we have not only found in the zeal for the Order and in the virtues that have long shone out in the actions of the Very High, very powerful, and very Excellent Prince GUSTAV III by the grace of God King of Sweden, of the Goths, and the Vandals, Heir of Norway, Duke of Schleswig-Holstein, Stormarn and Ditmarsh, Count of Oldenburg and of Delmenhorst, in Ordine Dicts: Equite de Corona Vindicata, all the qualities that we might wish for the good of the Order, but also that this Prince, whose House has for several centuries often been allied with ours, has been the only one of our family who has shown interest in our misfortune. Wishing therefore to show him our gratitude, this considered, we have declared, as we presently declare, that should we have the misfortune to leave behind us no legitimate male child, we have named, elected, and chosen the aforementioned GUSTAV III King of the Goths and Vandals as our Coadjutor and Successor in the hereditary Grand Mastery of the Holy Order of the Temple of Our Lord Jesus Christ, He and his male Successors to the Royal throne of Sweden, born to a legitimate marriage and admitted as Freemasons according to the laws of the Order, with all the rights, preroga-

tives, immunities, and power with which we and our predecessors have exercised this Dignity.

We order all those who are under our obedience, Provinces, their leaders, Directories, Grand Priors and other officers, Chapters and all the Knightly Brothers of the said Order, to recognize by virtue of these irrevocable patent letters the aforementioned Very High, Very Powerful, And Very Excellent Prince GUSTAV III, by the grace of God King of Sweden and of the Goths and Vandals, Heir of Norway, Duke of Schleswig-Holstein, Stormarn, and Ditmarsh, Count of Oldenburg and of Delmenhorst, in Ordine Dictum: Equitem de Corona Vindicata, as our Coadjutor in the Grand Mastery and after Our death as Sovereign Leader and hereditary Grand Master of the Order, and to obey him in this role, as the laws of the Order require.

By naming this Prince as our Successor, we fulfill the duty that our affection for the Order /demands of us and confirm this election, which we wish to be seen as our supreme, final, and irrevocable/ will on the sacred numbers of Three, Four, and Nine.

In witness whereof, we have signed the present papers in our hand and marked them with our seal

Signed in Florence, this December 8, MDCCLXXXIII

(□)
S[ign]*ed* \ [Masonic characters] + Charles

S[ign]*ed*\ knight
CMistowy

Gen^{al} Secretary +"

However, a witness[11] asserts that Gustav III was (justifiably!) disappointed not to find in his interlocutor the esoteric wisdom that Plommenfeldt had praised so highly. Perhaps he put it down to Charles Edward's age and to the illness that had weakened him so greatly.

Even though (or perhaps because) all of this was secret, the news traveled fast. In a letter to the Brothers of Strasbourg, Doctor Giraud, one of the Italian dignitaries of the Order, wrote on February 21, 1784, barely three months after the precious document was awarded:

> I bring you strange news that will make you laugh! Before the death of the Pretender [?] the King of Sweden went to see him, had several conferences with him, & finally asked him in exchange for the sum of a Thousand louis d'or for the resignation of his place of Grand Master of the Order of the T . . . , which the pretender resigned very willingly as you would imagine; & consequently he gave him a Patent, which Sweden will invoke.[12]

It was perhaps "news that will make you laugh" because everyone in Italy knew of Charles Edward's pitiful state. However, it is also possible that the laughter of Giraud and the Alsatian brothers was forced. Partisans of Ferdinand von Brunswick, they were fully aware of the advantage that the precious parchment gave his competitors. Learning of Gustav III's nomination as coadjutor,

Waechter rushed to Florence, counting on his good relationship with Charles Edward to defend the rights of Ferdinand von Brunswick. However, he did not arrive until April 1784, three months after Gustav's departure with his real Jacobite patent in hand![13] In the margin of the original of Giraud's letter, Brother de Turckeim has written:

> *Meiningen, May 15, 1784.[14]*

> *According to news from Rome, found in Gotha, the King of Sweden has not only bought the proclaimed or imaginary rights of the Stuart Prince to the General Grand Mastery of the Order, but the King himself has become a Roman Catholic, & had the Pope rehabilitate the Ancient O. of the T., of which the officers of the King's entourage openly wear, it is said, the little red cross on their clothes & therefore the entourage is once again bringing the Cross into the Grand Order of Sweden known as the Seraphs.*

The Swedish were quick to report their new title. The archives of the Province of Burgundy kept a copy of the following account:

> *The Grand Master of the Holy Order of the Knights of Saint John of the Temple of our Lord Jesus Christ names for his coadjutor G. A. [that is, Gustave Adolphe] in Ord. dictus Eques a Corona vindicata, by a patent that he sent to him when he was at his home in Florence on December 8, 1783.[15]*

---

[11] The Chevalier des Tours, who organized the meeting, cited by René Leforestier in *La Franc-Maçonnerie Occultiste et Templière*, 698n54.

[12] Transcribed and published in Maruzzi, *La Stretta Osservanza Templare*, 99.

[13] Elements reported by Frank McLynn based on the "Stuart Papers" kept at Windsor, in McLynn, *Charles Edward Stuart*, 535.

[14] Transcribed and published in Maruzzi, *La Stretta Osservanza Templare*, 100.

[15] Transcribed and published in Maruzzi, *La Stretta Osservanza Templare*, 100.

This patent is signed Brother Charles ✠.

The patent was read in the Chapter of the Masters of the Temple in S.[Stockholm] on March 22, 1785, and the record of this reading is signed Nicolaus Bielke ✠.

On the death of C: E: [Charles Edward Stuart] this piece was once again exhibited & approved, & placed on the protocol of the Chapter of the M[asters of the] T[emple] on April 18, 1788.

Written on it are the words:
Defuncto C. E. in Capitulo M. T. die 18 aprilis 1788 denuo exibitum & approbatum ut in protocollo.
Nicolaus Cornes Bielke +
M.C. IX.^{ae} Prov.^{ae}
Eques a Sole aureo succedit 1743. Moritur 31. Januar. 1788.
G... in ordine dictus Eques et Frater professus a Corona vindicata succedit 31. Januar. 1788. Agnoscitur a + [i. e. Capitulo] Can[onicorum] regul[arium] S[tockholm] 18. april. 1788.

Charles Edward was again questioned about the Stuarts' connections with Freemasonry in 1787. The Lutheran theologian Friedrich Münter visited him and asked him about the subject, but the conversation quickly faltered because Charles Edward was so weak.[16] When he died on January 31, 1788, by virtue of this authentic Jacobite Masonic patent, his "coadjutor" Gustav III, "Eques a Corona Vindicata," succeeded him as leader of the "Order of the Knights of Saint John of the Temple." Did the King

of Sweden nevertheless maintain some illusions about Charles Edward's Masonic powers? It is of course difficult to say. However, we know that as soon as he was informed of his death, he sent the Count of Fredenheim to his daughter in Italy. She gave him "a document in Latin" on July 19, 1788.[17]

This forgotten episode, where Freemasonry furtively meets the debris of major history, is highly curious. However, like many curiosities, far from being anecdotal, it highlights remarkable traits of human psychology. It tells, after all, of just how powerful an idea can be—even if it is false. Opinion was convinced that the Stuarts were the secret leaders of the Lodges, and they eventually became just that, admittedly in somewhat unusual and, in truth, rather funny circumstances.

Since time immemorial, the question "Are you a Freemason?" has been answered according to Masonic instructions with the words "My Brothers recognize me as such." Charles Edward had long been recognized "as such" by many Masons during the eighteenth century. As his life drew to an end, he eventually accepted this crown that everyone wanted to place on his head. The only crown he ever had.

---

[16] Element reported by Frank McLynn in *Charles Edward Stuart*, 548, according to Frederik Münter, *Aus den Tagebuchern Friedrich Munters wandrrund lajahre eines Danisken gelerthen*, 3 vols. (Copenhagen and Leipzig: P. Haase, 1937), 2:232.
[17] Nordmann, *Gustave III*, 220.

Ritual, Secrecy, and Civil Society - Volume 3 - Number 1 - Spring 2015

An Archaic "Scottish Master" at the Roots of High Degrees: The First High Degree Finally Revealed?

Pierre Mollier[A]

Since the eighteenth century, Freemasonry has used a double teaching system, and continues to do so today. Firstly, the Mason moves up through the degrees of Entered Apprentice, Fellowcraft, and Master. However, once they have achieved the grade of Master, those who want to continue their initiatory progression can move up through the high degrees. Although historians have now managed to reconstruct the sources and roots of the first three degrees in Great Britain from the seventeenth century to the 1730s, the origins of "Perfect Master," "Scottish Master," and "Royal Arch" remain rather mysterious. Admittedly, there has been significant progress in the history of the high degrees. They are no longer seen as a late, French creation, as was long the case, but as a phenomenon also rooted in the British effervescence of 1717 to1730, and therefore as coming directly in the wake of the formation of Speculative Freemasonry. Historians such as René Guilly had emphasized that the oldest high degrees—such as the "Royal Arch" (attested in Ireland in 1743) or the "Perfect Master" and the "Scottish Master" (both attested in Paris in 1744)—had points in common and seem to respond to the establishment of the "new" degree of Master in around 1730. Recently, the discovery of two documents has

allowed a new model to be proposed for the appearance of the high degrees. At the center of the process lies an archaic degree of "Scottish Master," about which we now have slightly more information. Might it even be the main source for this "Scottish Masonry" that flourished so vigorously in the eighteenth century?

A "Scottish Master" in London 1733

The first trace of a "Scottish Masonry" in the sense of high degrees (that is, with practices above the degree of Master) is from London in 1733. It tells of the existence of a "Scots Masons' Lodge," which met in the *Devil's Tavern*, where other Lodges—for example, the *Union Lodge*—also worked. The adjective "Scotts" clearly does not refer to the origin of the Brothers, some of whom we know were already Master Masons. The ceremony of "making and admitting [them as] Scottish Master Masons" therefore gave them an additional degree, distinct from that of "Master Mason." The archives reveal the existence of a few other Scottish Lodges, for example in Bath in 1735. There are therefore several incontestable accounts of a degree of "Scottish Master" being practiced between 1730 and 1740 in England. Bernard Jones, who has

---

[A] Director of the Grand Orient de France Library and of the Museum of Freemasonry (Paris).
[1] Roger Dachez, *Hiram et ses frères: Essai sur les origines du grade de Maître* (Paris: Véga, 2010).

doi: 10.18278/rscs.3.1.4

devoted a scholarly article to the issue, cites the great English historian Robert F. Gould, "who would have known some of the elements of the ritual" of these first Scottish Master Lodges, and according to whom this ritual was based on "the discovery of the Ineffable Word, lost long ago, in a crypt, by Scottish Crusaders." As with the Masonry of the first three degrees, this "Scottish" Masonry would follow the major currents of exchange, and soon established itself on the continent. Thus, in Paris in 1744, Abbé Pérau stated: "I am well aware that there is a vague rumor among Freemasons, concerning a certain order that they call the Scots, claimed to be superior to ordinary Freemasons & who have their own ceremonies and secrets." However, apart from a few rare and short accounts attesting without doubt to its existence, very little is known about this first degree of "Scottish Master."

An Italian Brother Brings the "Scottish Master" from London to Berlin in 1742

In 2000, the return from Russia of a part of the archives of the Grand Orient de France, which had been pillaged by the Nazis, revealed an essential document for the history of the high degrees: the register (over 150 pages long) of a Lodge of "Scottish Masters" who practiced in Berlin from 1742 to 1749. This very cosmopolitan Lodge was founded by an Italian, Brother Jacopo Fabris, and contained Brothers of various nationalities, many of whom were French. It even carried out its works in French. Yet Fabris, a tireless leader who at the first session received the six other founders of the grade of "Scottish Master," came from London. There he had been a member of the *Union Lodge*, which also met at the *Devil's Tavern*. Moreover, the register reports that

the Berlin Brothers were in contact with the London Brothers. Without making hasty connections, we can assume that this "Scottish Master" that Fabris established in Berlin in 1742 was not unrelated to the degree that he may have received in London in the Scots Masons' Lodge of the Devil's Tavern. He spent some of his evenings in this tavern. An additional element has recently been discovered, justifying the connection between the Scottish Lodges of London and Berlin. In the magnificent Kloss collection of the Grand Orient of the Netherlands, Jan Snoek and Pierre Noël found a mid-1740s copy of the ritual of the Scottish Lodge of Berlin. It clearly corresponds exactly to the words attributed to Gould, because it is based on "the discovery of the Ineffable Word, lost long ago, in a crypt, by Scottish Crusaders." It is therefore highly probable that the "Scottish Masonry" practiced in Berlin in 1742 was the same as that which appeared in London in 1733, and which was used by several "Scots Masons' Lodges" in England.

Following Jan Snoek and Pierre Noël's discovery, another researcher, Claude Weiler, drew our attention to a unique manuscript that complements and reinforces this hypothesis of a "source" Scottish degree. The unusual nature of the *Copiale* manuscript, discovered in 2011, makes it worthy of a dedicated article of its own. However, here we are very interested in the second, somewhat noncentral part, where the author describes Masonry in his time: around 1745 to 1750. Notably, he devotes several pages to the "Scottish Master." He states that there were two variants: French and German, and he gives many details about both. These elements considerably complete the Kloss manuscript, which although fascinating, remained allusive and even incomplete on several points. It should be noted that the two versions of the "Scottish Master" (the

Copiale manuscript even proposes a third) show great similarities, and are clearly derived from a common source. The author of the *Copiale* manuscript even comments that the Scottish Lodges have "similar, if not identical, ceremonies." When these three documents are examined together, they probably give a fairly representative image of the first high degree of Scottish Master.

A Primitive Form of the Degree of the Royal Arch

I will now attempt to piece together this early Scottish Masonry, much as an archaeologist might restore a large fresco by repositioning various remains of mosaics. In the degree of Master, the legend of Hiram tells us that the true word of the Master was lost when the architect of the Temple died. In the degree of Scottish Master, this true word, which is more substantial because it is the name of God himself, is found again:

> *When the Scottish knights . . . were working together to reconstruct the temple of the Almighty in Jerusalem, when they were rebuilding the foundations of the old Temple, this holy place that some call very holy, they found buried there three cubes and three rounded stones, which were the true foundation stones. The knights, who were Masons, went into the greatest ecstasy when they saw under the last stone the word of J . . . or A . . . , which was the true word of the master. They lifted this stone with the greatest care and took it from the holy land on their return to Scotland.*

In the remains of the Temple of Solomon during the work to rebuild it, they found buried in the foundations an essential stone bearing the name of God—the true "word of the Master," which had been lost. This is the symbolic theme of the "Royal Arch." Of course, an arch is not yet formally mentioned, but this strange stone certainly has the appearance of a keystone, and it was found in the foundations of the Temple. Following on from Gould's observation, Bernard Jones added that if the elements were confirmed, then "from 1733, the Lodge at the *Devil's Tavern* must have practiced a primitive form of the degree of the Royal Arch." We can now say that this was the case.

The Origins of the Perfect Master

However, this first high degree of "Scottish Master" was symbolically very rich: so rich that it would be divided into several degrees. Thus, alongside the Royal Arch, the "Perfect Master" (one of the first high degrees attested in France) also appeared as a breakaway of the first Scottish Master. The general atmosphere of the Lodge was almost the same: omnipresence of the color green and a systematic use of the symbolic number four (four candlesticks, four trips, and so forth). But above all, the latter element gave the Perfect Master the unique symbol that came to be its mark: a curious motif of four circles in four squares, on top of two columns in a saltire forming a St. Andrew's Cross, with the letter J for Jehovah in the middle. It is worth noting in passing that René Guilly's analysis, which sees this as an emblem of the "Foundation Stone" of Jewish legend, is confirmed by this source document, as the ritual of Scottish Master explains that they are the "true foundation stones." It symbolizes the stone that Yahweh threw into the *Chao* as a foundation for Creation and that Jewish legends place in the depths of the Earth but vertically aligned with the Holy of Holies of the Temple of Jerusalem.

The New Levite "Scottish Master"

After comparing the Kloss manuscript and the descriptions of the ritual in the *Copiale*, we now have quite a precise picture of reception into this first degree of Scottish Master. Candidates to become a Master enter the Scottish Lodge in a position of humility, with a rope around their neck. They must circle the tracing board four times in a silence broken only by the blow of a mallet, and the quiet pronunciation of each of the first three degrees on each circuit. On the fourth circuit, they are purified with water from the basin placed on a small table beside the Bible. The discourse explains that when working in the ruins of the Temple, the Scottish Masters found the ancient word of the Master that had been lost when Hiram died. This word is nothing less than God's true name. The instruction gives the symbolic meaning of the reception:

> Q. Where were you received?
> A. In the Holy of Holies, under the acacia.
> Q. What did you see in the Temple of Solomon?
> A. The Ark of the Covenant, and the sea on the twelve cattle.
> Q. What is the purpose of the sea?
> A. To purify the Levites.

Upon receiving the degree of Scottish Master, the Mason was made a Levite: a preacher serving the Temple, admitted into the Holy of Holies, and put in possession of God's true name! We cannot help but detect a priestly dimension to this first high degree.

The Source of Scottish Masonry

As well as being a direct source for two of the oldest and most important high degrees in Masonic tradition, the "Royal Arch" and the "Perfect Master," our first Scottish Master displays other symbols and legends that recur in many of the high degrees of the eighteenth century, starting with the reference to Knighthood, because it was "Scottish Knights" who found God's true name in the ruins of the Temple during the Crusades. Sometimes at the end of the ceremony, and sometimes several months afterwards, the new Scottish Masters would be dubbed "Knights of the Scottish Order." If, as we think, all of this does come from London, Ramsay did not "invent" the chivalric ancestry of Freemasonry: he really only developed and popularized an idea that was already present in early Speculative Freemasonry. We should remember that the connection with Knighthood is already drafted out in Anderson's *Constitutions* of 1723, and evoked in several British texts from the 1720s.

With the Berlin ritual of "Scottish Master" from 1742 and the explanations given by the *Copiale*, we probably hold one of the most important pieces in the puzzle concerning the origin of the high degrees. However, the images are undeniably unclear, if we take into account the other elements regarding the "high degrees:" the attestation of the Order of Heredom of Kilwinning in London in 1741, the problem of the secret installation of the Master, and quite simply the already very different versions of the degree of Scottish Master in the second half of the 1740s. The *Copiale* tells us that at this time there were the French Scottish Lodge, the Scottish Lodges of Berlin and Brunswick, and "the other Scottish Lodges of Germany." They certainly display many similarities, but also significant differences: the color of the French Scottish Master is not green but red, everything is in threes rather than fours, and so forth.

Perhaps the inconsistencies between these different accounts are the traces of an original practice when the transmission of degrees did not yet take place via a "fully formed," highly structured ceremony. Certain elements would therefore suggest that at the very beginnings of Speculative Freemasonry, the stages of a Mason's career would have been marked by symbolic dialogues, in which the recipient had to participate, around a tracing board placed on a table. This much more flexible form naturally encourages a rapid enriching of the dialogues and commentaries. It is only in a second stage that this symbolic material would have been split into separate and structured ceremonies, with opening, reception, instruction, and closing rituals. This would explain both the deep similarities and the significant differences between the different versions of the rituals, since they did not become fixed in exactly the same way in different Masonic environments. Our first Scottish Masters might therefore have been derived from a great original dialogue on the discovery of the ruins and the reconstruction of the Temple of Jerusalem.

Freemasonry and Orientalism[1]

Thierry Zarcone[A]

That the Orient lies deep within masonic mythology is evidenced in the most ancient rituals of the Order; this reference has a particular influence on the conduct of freemasons towards this Orient, whether it is internalized as an ideal place to be found within oneself, or externalized in the form of a real "oriental journey." We can therefore understand why, to sum up the spirit of the earliest masonic texts, an English freemason could write in 1860 that "[i]n the East the Science had its origin; from the East first came Religion, and the Arts and Sciences, and to the East the Craftman is yet directed to look as the source of all light."[2] This is the reason why we may say that the masonic project is in essence "orientalist." Thus, the contact of freemasons with the world of the East, whether as an intellectual adventure or an actual journey, could not be recounted better than by those who were indeed specialists in this part of the world, its languages, history, customs and literature, that is, the literature of "dragomans"[3], diplomats, and orientalists. By "orientalist" we here mean historians, geographers, anthropologists, and sociologists who have mastered sources in oriental languages, not only philologists.

Although the term "Orient" generally refers to the Levant, that is, the Ottoman Empire, and more specifically its borders with the eastern Mediterranean, with the freemasons it took on different meanings according to the eras to which they were referring or the precise spiritual tradition to which their rites relate. The first of these Orients is Egypt where freemasons sought the footsteps of Hermes / Toth.[4] *The Old Charges*, in particular the Regius (fourteenth century) and the Cooke (fifteenth century) manuscripts, locate the origins of the order in Egypt and mention the names of the philosophers Euclid, who caused Geometry to be considered the art of builders, and Hermes (Trismegistus), the eponymous founder of hermeticism, together with a few other biblical figures. The second Orient dear to masons is the Holy Land where they dream of reliving the biblical story of the construction of the Temple of Solomon and that of the Last Supper.

[A] Thierry Zarcone (PhD, Habilitation) is director of researches at the CNRS, based at the Ecole Pratique des Hautes Etudes (Sorbonne). He teaches also at the School of Political Sciences (Aix-en-Provence) the history and anthropology of Islam in Turkey and in the Mediterranean.

[1] This article is a corrected and extended version of the section on "Orientalism" in the *Dictionnaire de la Franc-maçonnerie*, ed. Pierre-Yves Beaurepaire (Paris: Armand Colin, 2014), 199–203.

[2] Samuel Laurence, *The Moral Design of Freemasonry deduced from the Old Charges of a free mason* (New York: Macoy, Sickel and Co., 1860), 209.

[3] Dragomans are local interpreters.

[4] See Charles Porset, "Le Voile de Saïs. L'Egypte des francs-maçons," in *Traces de l'Autre. Mythes de l'Antiquité et Peuples du Livre dans la construction des nations méditerranéennes*, ed. Josiane Boulad-Ayoub and Gian Mario Cazzaniga (Paris: Pisa, Jean Vrin, 2004), 27–40.

doi: 10.18278/rscs.3.1.5

Finally, a third Orient, from the nineteenth century, is, perhaps surprisingly, the "Plateau of Tartary" (that is, central Asia) to which we must even add the Indies.[5] We know, for example, that for countless freemasons and Russian esotericists, the city of Astrakhan on the Caspian Sea, inhabited by Tatars, was considered, from the eighteenth century, to be the gateway to the East. [6]

The masonic ideal therefore extended beyond the eastern Mediterranean which was its legendary birthplace; it was reinforced by all the many forms that the idea of the Orient could take, and it never ceased extending ever more towards the East, as the Levant became better known and less mysterious. The details of how the masons invented this third Orient do have some interest for us. We read in the journal *L'Univers maçonnique (The Masonic World)*, in 1835, that "the most careful writers place its birthplace [that of freemasonry] in the land that was probably the first to be inhabited, that is, the *Plateau of Tartary*, and have passed it down to us via the sages of India, Persia, Ethiopia and Egypt."[7] Another article in the same journal gives further details of this *Plateau of Tartary* where freemasonry first arose. Its author states that:

> from the first appearance of Tartary in history, we find it with kans and lamas; religious superstitions defile the worship we owe to the creator, and the freedom of the peoples is oppressed by the political power instituted to defend it; but sages gather in the deserts or on isolated banks of the Oxus to agree upon how to give reason back

its debased rights, and guarantee once more national independence.

These sages, writes the author, created an "institute" which turned out to be the original form of freemasonry: "The institute of these first masons became regularized; it began to have mysterious meetings in places where the foundations of the city of Samarkand were later laid . . ." Then the institute concerned brought justice and tolerance to that country where the "kans" were the politicians, and the "lama" were the priests, and "soon there were affiliates in every part of the known world of that time. Fortunate, forever fortunate, was the time that saw the meeting of Isis, Thaut, and Zoroaster." And our author adds that these great spirits "turned to the Tartars, who were then confused with the Indians, to draw on the principles of those institutions whose wisdom we still admire today." In this way, Isis and Thaut (Hermes in fact) came from Egypt, and Zoroaster from Iran, to be instructed in this Tartar wisdom before returning home. Finally, the author explains, it was thanks to Isis that "masonry, whose model Isis had found in the peoples of Tartary" was passed on to the West.[8] This legend of the origins of the masonic order then shows how the Jews and Christians in their turn obtained this wisdom. This myth of origins is unusual in that it locates the origin of the masonic order in Greater Asia.

The great majority of the dragomans were Eastern, generally Christians, Greeks or Armenians, and Moslems in India, those of European origin being very rare. Their relationship to freemasonry was often a professional necessity since belonging to

---

[5] Brother Chemin-Dupontès and Anonymous, "Examen des différentes opinions sur l'origine de la franc-maçonnerie," *L'Univers maçonnique* 1 (1835): 4, 214–215.

[6] Gérald Duverdier, "L'Orientalisme piétiste en Prusse et en Russie," *Dix-Huitième siècle* 28 (1996): 85–88.

[7] Brother Chemin-Dupontès, "Examen des différentes opinion sur l'origine de la franc-maçonnerie," *L'Univers maçonnique* 1 (1835): 4.

[8] Anonymous, "Recherches statistiques sur la franc-maçonnerie," *L'Univers maçonnique* 1 (1835): 214–215

the Order allowed them to frequent diplomats and merchants and to fraternize with them. Towards the end of the eighteenth century and the beginning of the nineteenth the dragomans gave way to European diplomats/interpreters. The most skillful of them divided their time between diplomacy and university life, and some even practiced both these careers, either simultaneously or in succession. As a diplomat, the orientalist and his knowledge were, however, commanded by their country, in the service of its imperialist policy. Several became active in this "orientalism," denounced by Edward Saïd,[9] which established the intellectual supremacy of the West, allowing a decadent East to be put under trusteeship.

From 1798 to 1811, the Egyptian Campaign gave the orientalists and academics who accompanied Napoleon's armies the opportunity to study this country with the aim of dominating it in knowledge and science. Among the nine orientalists who were to take part in this campaign and who *de facto* belonged to the commission for the arts and sciences, one was a freemason and three others were to become one a few years later: these were Henri-Nicolas Belleteste (1778–1808), Louis-Rémy Raige (1777–1810), Pierre-Amédée Jaubert (1779–1847), and Jean-Baptiste L'Homaca. The latter, a Greek dragoman, was a member of a lodge belonging to the network of the Scottish Mother Lodge from Marseille to Constantinople, in 1766–1768. Belleteste and Raige later contributed to the famous

Description de l'Egypte (1809–1828). Together with Jaubert, who was to become a teacher of Persian at the Collège de France, they belonged in Paris to the Saint-Jean d'Ecosse du Grand Sphinx Lodge (1804), along with a great number of academics, including several members of the Institute, and soldiers, all veterans of the Egyptian Campaign. When Belleteste died in 1808, we read that his funeral eulogy, which was given at the Lodge of *Saint-Jean d'Ecosse du Grand Sphinx* included the following: "He dedicated himself entirely to the study of history and oriental languages, and he obtained all the success one could desire. He was not yet twenty when he was chosen to be part of the Commission of arts and sciences which accompanied the French army to Egypt."[10] The masonic ideal gave new life, in that lodge, to the emblems and symbols of the Egypt of the Pharaohs, and the orientalists of the *Great Sphinx* implicitly supported the idea that the Egyptian Orient was the land where freemasonry originated. Sylvestre de Sacy (1758–1838), an iconic figure in orientalism and a freemason in the Scottish Mother Lodge in France, added, from his Chair as Professor in the new School of Modern Oriental Languages, that there were surprising analogies between the ancient Mysteries, those of Mithra in particular, and freemasonry.[11]

On the other hand, the orientalists brought competition to the Scottish Mother Lodge of France where in 1809, with the encouragement of the imperial power, the

---

[9] Edward Saïd, *Orientalism* (New York: Pantheon, 1978).

[10] *Funeral eulogy for Henri-Nicolas Belleteste, secretary/interpreter to the Government for oriental languages, and member of the Institute of Egypt, given in the R∴[espectable] L∴[odge] of Great Sphinx, on the 20th∴ day of the 8th∴ month 5808 (Common Era: October 20, 1808)*, by the V∴[enerable] F∴[Brother] Henri Duval, p. 5. See the notice by Pierre Mollier on Belleteste in *L'Etat-major maçonnique de Napoléon, dictionnaire biographique des dirigeants du Grand Orient de France sous le Premier Empire*, ed. Pierre Mollier and Pierre-François Pinaud (Orleans, France: Editions A l'Orient, 2009), 85.

[11] See Thierry Zarcone, "The 'Secret Life' of Sylvestre de Sacy (Orientalism in Freemasonry)," *Ritual, Secrecy and Civil Society* 2 (2) (Winter 2014): 93-107.

envoy of the shah of Iran, Askari Khan,[12] was initiated. In fact, Napoleon badly needed the support of Persia against the British in his plan to conquer India. Similarly, the orientalists linked to English freemasonry served British imperialism in India, and later the French orientalist freemasons embarked on their mission to civilize their land (mission civilisatrice) in North Africa. The prominent figure in Algeria was Joanny Pharaon (1803–1846), a member, like his father Elias Pharaon (1774–1827), of the Masonic Order."[13] The latter was Napoleon Bonaparte's interpreter during the Egyptian Campaign, and Joanny Pharaon was interpreter to the Governor General of Algeria. As a historian of France and the Arab world, specializing in Islamic law, he held the professorial Chair of Arabic in Algiers and published the first grammar of this language in 1830. In his study of the Kabyles published in 1835, he described the difficulties encountered by the French in "civilizing" these people, a sign that his orientalism was in the service of the French state.[14] The academic thus reinforced, through his work, the civilizing and *de facto* colonialist project which had the support of almost all the French freemasons in Algeria.

The masonic commitment of the orientalists also led some of them to question the symbolic Orient of their ritual as well as the relationship of this legendary *topos* with the geographical Orient they were studying and in which they were evolving. Their works show how the orientalist freemason saw the Eastern Christian, Muslim or Hindu world, and whether this view was able to inspire or mark their brothers in the Order and help these to know their symbolic Orient better. Nevertheless, only a few orientalists expressed an opinion on this subject, as most of them, no doubt for ethical reasons, never dealt with freemasonry in relation to the subject of their study.

The main view the freemason orientalists had of the Orient may be described as perennialist or supraconfessionnal. The Orient is recognized as the place where all religions discover for themselves a universal spiritual ideal and freemasonry as the instrument of an extreme ecumenism which encourages the overlooking of denominational divisions. This attitude is clearly embodied by the Russian Gerasim Lebedev (1749–1817) who lived in India for fourteen years, wrote the first Hindustani grammar book and translated parts of the *Baghavad Gita*. Supported by freemasons close to the tsar and initiated into a British lodge in India, he did not interpret Hinduism as polytheism but as Proto-Christianity; for Lebedev, the objective of freemasonry was to go beyond the reunification of just the separate branches of Christianity, towards the union of all religions.[15]

This perennialism explains above all the links established by several orientalist

---

[12] Thierry Zarcone, "Comment peut-on être Persan et franc-maçon ? L'ambassadeur Askeri Khan à Paris en 1808-1810 ",in Jean Scot Érigène, *Les Cahiers Jean Scot Érigène*, No. 8 (Paris: Grande Loge de France, 2009), 183–197.

[13] A higher diploma was awarded in 1820 to Elias Pharaon. (I thank Pierre Mollier for drawing my attention to this document; it is preserved in the archives of the Grand Orient of France.) On the affiliation of Joanny Pharaon to freemasonry, see Xavier Yacono, *Un Siècle de franc-maçonnerie algérienne* (1785–1884) (Paris: Maisonneuve et Larose, 1969), 74. On both these men see Alain Messaoudi, "Orientaux orientalistes, les Pharaon, interprètes du Sud au service du Nord," in *Sud-Nord. Cultures coloniales en France (XIXe–XXe siècles)*, ed. Colette Zytnicki and Chantal Bordes-Benayoun (Toulouse, France: Privat, 2004), 243–255.

[14] Joanny Pharaon and Florian Joanny, *Les Cabiles et Boudgie* (Algiers: Philippe, 1835), 89.

[15] Yaroslav Vassilkov, "From the History of Indian Studies in Russia: Gerasim Lebedev and the Freemasons," *Studia Orientalia* 110 (2011): 317–330.

masons, from the end of the eighteenth century up to recent years, on the basis of their work, between freemasonry and the Sufi brotherhoods (*tarîqa*) of the Muslim world. The Armenian Catholic Ignatius Muradgea d'Ohsson (1740–1807), a dragoman in the service of the Swedish and French legations, attached to lodges related to these two countries and author of a famed history of the Ottoman Empire, was the first to recognize the Sufis as "Oriental Freemasons." He was followed in the nineteenth century by John P. Brown (1812–1872), an American diplomat, Grand Master of the District Grand Lodge of Turkey (United Grand Lodge of England) and author of a great classic on Sufism (*The Darvishes or Oriental Spiritualism*, 1868), which calls the dervishes "Mussulman Freemasons." At approximately the same time, Sir Richard Burton (1821–1890), who was received into freemasonry in Lahore, India, and a specialist in the Indian sub-continent, went as far as to convert to Islam and subscribed to Sufism; he wrote that the dervishes were a type of "Oriental freemasonry."[16] More recently, the professor of political science Bruno Etienne (1937–2009), a member of the Grand Orient de France, high dignitary of the Supreme Council of the Ancient Accepted Scottish Rite and specialist in the world of Islam, put a new slant on this issue which became: "freemasonry, a western

tariqa." His aim was to make Western freemasons aware that their type of sociability was very similar to that of the Sufi brotherhoods and that they could take inspiration from the latter to slow down the corruption of their "tradition."[17] More surprisingly, the orientalist Henry Corbin (1903–1978), a specialist in philosophy and in the Shiite Gnosis, who was then a member of the French National Grand Lodge, shortly before his death and with the utmost discretion, along with some freemasons such as the editor Jean de Foucault and the anthropologist Gilbert Durand, drew up a ritual with a Christian character entitled the "Abrahamic rite" or the "rite of Melchisedech" which is based both on freemasonry and on the Order of the Knights Templar. Corbin's works on Persian Sufism were referred to at times during the creation of this ritual.[18]

This perennialist vision had the consequence of encouraging the recruitment of candidates who were not Christian into the lodges; it was at the instigation of the Spaniard Alexis Gierra, formerly of the Army of the Orient and a specialist in Greek and Arab languages, that many Easterners, including Muslims, were therefore received into the lodges in Marseille at the beginning of the nineteenth century.[19] But orientalists were divided on the role that the Orient should play at that time in the spreading

---

[16] On Brown and Burton see Thierry Zarcone, "French Pre-Masonic Fraternities, Freemasonry and Dervish Orders in the Muslim World," in *Freemasonry and Fraternalism in the Middle East*, ed. Andreas Önnerfors and Dorothe Sommer (Sheffield, UK: University of Sheffield, 2008), 35–36.

[17] See my analysis in "Sociabilités en miroir : de la loge maçonnique à la confrérie soufie," in *Bruno Etienne, le fait religieux comme fait politique*, ed. Franck Frégosi (La Tour d'Aigues, France: L'Aube, 2009), 270–283.

[18] According to a letter from Corbin dated September 18, 1972, and the rituals of this rite communicated by Antoine Faivre (2011) and Robert Salmon (2014).

[19] Mathieu Grenet, "La Loge et l'étranger: Les Grecs dans la franc-maçonnerie marseillaise dans le premier quart du XIXe siècle," *Cahiers de la Méditerranée* 72 (June 2006): 236–237, and "Alexis Gierra, 'interprète juré des langues orientales' à Marseille: une trajectoire entre marchands, frères et refugiés (fin XVIIIe-premier tiers du XIXe siècle)," in *Langues et langages du commerce en Méditerranée et en Europe à l'époque moderne*, ed. Gilbert Buti, Michèle Janin-Thivos, and Olivier Raveux (Aix-en-Provence, France: Presses Universitaires de Provence, 2013), 57–58.

of the masonic "light." Some thought that the world of the East could still guide the freemasons in their quest for truth, that they possessed timeless wisdom, but others considered that, on the contrary, the "light," previously acquired in the East had then been preserved in the West, and that it was now being reintroduced by the Europeans to the lands where it had been lost:

> The light came to us in former times from the East; we now return to you a few rays which we have preserved since time immemorial, in the midst of storms that would have extinguished them. It is now up to you to make of them a new flame for which the earth has need.[20]

The "civilizing mission" (mission civilisatrice) of the French in North Africa was given legitimacy by the freemasons in the name of this interpretation.

There was still an attitude—even though it was uncommon—that was diametrically opposed to the perennialist vision. This attitude developed within a freemasonry that was said to be in the Christian tradition and whose ultimate aim was a symbolic, or mystical, experience of Christ. This was the case with the German and Scandinavian Christian Freemasonries and the Rectified Scottish Rite in France. The most suggestive example was that of Julius Heinrich Petermann (1801–1876), a theologian, Armenian specialist, and professor extraordinaire of Eastern literature at the University of Berlin, who undertook research in Jerusalem in 1868 while occupying a post as a Prussian diplomat. Petermann was a member of a Berlin lodge of the Grand Lodge of Prussia (Grosse Loge v. Prussengen "Royal York zur Freundschaft"), and maintained that the mission of freemasonry was "a mission for promoting true Christianity"; he then added that freemasons "are obliged to prepare the work for the Missionaries, because the true and genuine Mason, in my opinion, must be a true and genuine Christian."[21]

Finally, the orientalist had the skills necessary for correcting or nuancing false ideas which freemasons might have developed about the oriental world and its links with freemasonry. The most memorable debate concerned the links between the freemasons and the Druze of Lebanon (a secret religion of Ismaili origin) by the intermediary of the Templars.[22] Supported by the German orientalist von Hammer Purgstall (1774–1856), who was an enemy of the freemasons, this theory was long advanced by freemasons seeking an oriental line of descent. It was rejected at the beginning of the nineteenth century by Sylvestre de Sacy, but nevertheless continued to inspire the freemasons of the following centuries. In another area, Joseph Anton von Bianchi d'Alba, an Iranist and member of a lodge in Vienna, corrected, in 1784, in the *Journal für Freymaurer* the opinions of his fellow masons concerning the influence of the Mysteries of Mithra on the ritual of masonic initiation.[23]

---

[20] *Le Véritable lien des peuples ou la franc-maçonnerie rendue à ses vrais principes. Recueil fait par un Européen pour l'instruction des loges qui se sont établies dans l'Asie et dans l'Inde au commencement du XIXe siècle*, circa 5829 [1829].

[21] Robert Morris, *Freemasonry in the Holy Land* (New York: Masonic Publishing Company, 1875), 470.

[22] On this question see Daniel de Smet, "Les Prétendues Origines druzes de la Franc-maçonnerie. Naissance et persistance d'un mythe," in *Traces de l'Autre*, 261–274.

[23] See the study of this journal by Jan Assmann in *Religio Duplex. Comment les lumières ont réinventé la religion des Egyptiens* (Paris: Aubier, 2013).

One will remember that the works and thoughts of the orientalist freemasons on the geographical Orient reveal an essential link between the masonic ideal and the Eastern world. This link led to two intellectual and political actions among European freemasons: an understanding of the self through the other and a fraternization with that other who, considered as an embodiment of wisdom, was to take the role of spiritual master, or, seen as a decadent ignoramus, had to be "civilized."

www.ingramcontent.com/pod-product-compliance
Lightning Source LLC
Chambersburg PA
CBHW081652270326
41933CB00018B/3442